PRAISE FOR *PROMISES KEPT*

How are Christians to understand the Old Testament covenants, and how do they relate to Christ? These are among the most pressing questions believers face, and Courtney Reissig offers a timely resource for Christians in this important Bible study, *Promises Kept*. Every believer and every congregation or Bible study group will find great encouragement, edification, wisdom, and faithfulness in this study of God's Word. This is an outstanding resource, and I commend it highly.

R. ALBERT MOHLER, JR.
President, The Southern Baptist Theological Seminary

Promises Kept walks you through the big picture of God's redemptive story in a way that will lead your heart to worship as you stand in awe of His faithfulness.

RUTH CHOU SIMONS
Wall Street Journal bestselling author, artist, and founder of gracelaced.com

Too many of us approach the Bible as if it contains two opposing halves: the Old Testament and the New Testament. Law and grace. Angry God, nice Jesus. This perspective is common, and unfortunate, because it misses the true relationship between the Old Testament and the New, which is *symmetry*. Jesus' life and teachings are constantly calling back to the Law and the Prophets in the most subtle and breathtaking ways, but we will miss all that is happening before our very eyes unless we have teachers to guide us. Thankfully, Courtney Reissig is just such a guide, illuminating the beauty and the depths of God's Word in both accessible and practical ways. This is a wonderful resource!

SHARON HODDE MILLER
Author of *The Cost of Control: Why We Crave It, the Anxiety It Gives Us, and the Real Power God Promises*

Covenants can be one of the most confusing and complex aspects of Scripture, but Courtney breaks them down with the skill and clarity of an experienced Bible teacher. With the use of simple timelines and charts, inductive study questions, thoughtful personal application, and opportunities for Scripture memory, students of the Word will come away with a deeper understanding of each covenant. I'm grateful for Courtney's work on this as she keeps the gospel narrative in focus and always points us to Christ!

EMILY JENSEN
Coauthor of *Risen Motherhood: Gospel Hope for Everyday Moments*

The Bible is full of endless riches that display the beauty of our God, and in *Promises Kept*, Courtney Reissig has given us an excellent resource to dig into some of these riches, specifically the trustworthiness of God. If you want to better understand the connection of the Old Testament to the New Testament and the bigger picture of what God has done, you'll love this Bible study! I certainly did.

CHRISTINE HOOVER
Bible teacher and author of *Seek First the Kingdom: God's Invitation to Life and Joy in the Book of Matthew*

The story of the Bible is the true story of the world. At the heart of that story is that God has been faithful to keep His promises. In *Promises Kept*, Courtney does a fantastic job of laying out the story of the Bible in beautiful and accessible ways so that everyone can behold the faithfulness of God to His people.

JT ENGLISH
Pastor, professor, and author of *Deep Discipleship: How the Local Church Can Make Whole Disciples*; cofounder of Training the Church; cohost of the *Knowing Faith* podcast

5 OLD TESTAMENT COVENANTS
AND HOW CHRIST FULFILLED THEM

A 6-WEEK BIBLE STUDY

PROMISES KEPT

COURTNEY REISSIG

MOODY PUBLISHERS

CHICAGO

Edited by Pamela Joy Pugh
Interior design: Kaylee Dunn
Cover design: Greg Jackson / Thinkpen Design
Cover illustration of watercolor copyright © 2022 by Alexander Evgenyevich / Shutterstock (637367359). All rights reserved.
Author photo: Lydia Singleton

Library of Congress Cataloging-in-Publication Data

Names: Reissig, Courtney, 1983- author.
Title: Promises kept : 5 Old Testament covenants and how Christ fulfilled
    them a 6-week Bible study / Courtney Reissig.
Description: Chicago : Moody Publishers, [2023] | Includes bibliographical
    references. | Summary: "The author takes students through five Old
    Testament covenants-promises-with the goal of seeing God's beautiful
    storyline. During these six weeks, participants see God's purposes for
    His people, their place in His purposes, and how the entire Bible fits
    together. Additionally, we'll see how Jesus fulfills God's loving
    covenants"-- Provided by publisher.
Identifiers: LCCN 2022037584 (print) | LCCN 2022037585 (ebook) | ISBN
    9780802428950 (paperback) | ISBN 9780802474452 (ebook)
Subjects: LCSH: Covenant theology. | Covenants. | BISAC: RELIGION /
    Biblical Studies / Old Testament / General | RELIGION / Biblical Studies
    / General
Classification: LCC BT155 .R36 2023 (print) | LCC BT155 (ebook) | DDC
    231.7/6--dc23/eng/20221115
LC record available at https://lccn.loc.gov/2022037584
LC ebook record available at https://lccn.loc.gov/2022037585

Originally delivered by fleets of horse-drawn wagons, the affordable paperbacks from D. L. Moody's publishing house resourced the church and served everyday people. Now, after more than 125 years of publishing and ministry, Moody Publishers' mission remains the same—even if our delivery systems have changed a bit. For more information on other books (and resources) created from a biblical perspective, go to www.moodypublishers.com or write to:

Moody Publishers
820 N. LaSalle Boulevard
Chicago, IL 60610

1 3 5 7 9 10 8 6 4 2

Printed in the United States of America

CONTENTS

STORIES MATTER

Have you ever started a story midway through and found yourself completely confused? The characters are compelling, but you have no idea what is going on. You could piecemeal the storyline with a few conversations here or a few plot twists there, but your understanding of the action as a whole is deficient. You need the entire story from beginning to end to understand what is really going on. Without this, the creator's purpose is completely lost on you.

I love Marvel movies. If someone wants to do a deep dive into the MCU (Marvel Cinematic Universe), I'm always down for that. But early on I took some liberties with watching the movies and watched them out of order. I thought it wouldn't matter.

It totally mattered.

I could figure out some of the details, but the major plot was lost on me because I skipped ahead. I needed to grasp the bigger story to understand the middle of the story. I learned my lesson that Marvel movies must be watched in order if I want to truly get the story.

This is even truer for the Bible. The Bible is one continuous story, but that is easy for us to forget because it is filled with so many different books and even books written in various genres: narrative, poetry, history, and so on. We find an abundance of characters. We can even spot stories within the story. It is hard for us to see how the content of Leviticus has anything to do with the narrative in 1 Samuel. I mean, does it?

I became a Christian in college but had grown up in a Christian home. Even though I didn't profess personal faith in Christ, the Bible was around. I was Bible-adjacent, you could say. So when God got ahold of me right before my twenty-first birthday, reading my Bible became a given. Shortly after, I asked my dad how to read the Bible. *Do I just read it like any other book? Where do I start? How often should I read it?*

Maybe you've asked similar questions. Everyone is different, but for me, it worked to just read it like a book. My dad told me that if I read four chapters a day, I could complete the whole Bible in a year. I started in Genesis and just started reading. But like all Bible reading plans, it got a little confusing around Leviticus, and super confusing at Judges. *What's with all these laws? Why are people so crazy? Is this really in the Bible?* So I went back to my dad with my questions and he gave me a commentary. I kept reading and kept studying.

Fast-forward a few years when I went to seminary. There I learned that the Bible is not just a book filled with isolated stories, but one big story. People use words like *overarching* and *metanarrative* to describe the continued storyline of the Bible. The book of Judges, for example, really does have a lot to do with the rest of the Bible. And the New Testament only makes sense in light of the Old Testament.

This began my journey toward not just reading the Bible but gaining tools to actually interpret the Bible and read it within its context and larger story. But maybe you've gotten this far and thought, *I'm not in seminary. I don't have time for seminary. I barely have time to read maybe a psalm or a few chapters of another book each day, let alone understand a whole context!*

I totally get it.

My seminary days are long over. Now my days are filled with carpool, meal prep, raising four boys, and working for my church. As much as I love spending hours reading and studying, the reality of my life is that I squeeze this activity into the margins. But when we lay out our days, we all can find space for the things that are important to us. There is nothing more important than our walk with the Lord.

Over the years, I have led and participated in a number of Bible studies. With each study, the most helpful things for me were clarity, expectations, and realism. A study that is realistic in what can be accomplished in my life, while also clearly telling me what to expect through the study, helped me believe I could succeed—both as a leader and a participant. That's what I hope this study does for you.

"God's Word is simple—all of us can understand it by the power of the Holy Spirit. It's also gloriously complex—we can spend a lifetime in it and never fully mine its depths."

Sometimes we come to the text thinking we can't understand it if we don't spend a lifetime studying it. But God's Word is simple—all of us can understand it by the power of the Holy Spirit. It's also gloriously complex—we can spend a lifetime in it and never fully mine its depths. The interpretive method in this study is designed to help you get as much as you'd like to from it.

I hope by the end of this study you will see that every book of the Bible is deeply connected to the one that came before it, and the one that comes after it. The Bible is one continuous portrait about God and His purposes in the world. As one theologian says, the Bible is telling the story of "God's people, in God's place, under God's rule."[1] We study the story of Scripture because we want to know how God has revealed Himself. This study is designed to help you see how the story unfolds, so you have some hooks to hang your understanding of the Bible on. It's also designed to help you see how you are deeply connected to this one story. If you're trusting in Christ, it is your story too.

GRASPING THE WHOLE STORY OF SCRIPTURE

Maybe you're asking this question: "So, what *is* the whole story of Scripture?" You might know individual stories in Scripture, like David and Goliath or Moses and the burning bush, but if you have never heard the Bible described in a way that connects them all, that's okay. That's what this study is for! The whole story of Scripture (think of those words *metanarrative* and *overarching*) is composed of four basic parts:

1. **Creation:** God created everything.
2. **Fall:** Humanity disobeyed our Creator and fell into sin.
3. **Redemption:** God promised a Redeemer to save His people from their sin— that Redeemer is Jesus Christ.
4. **Consummation:** Jesus promises to return one day, making all things right.

In every part of the Bible, we should be asking "Where is Christ?" and "Where am I?" in this narrative. The Bible is a progressive story, in which each book of the Bible functions like a chapter, moving the story forward. It is progressing toward a planned end. In the Old Testament, it's moving us toward the birth, death, and resurrection of Jesus Christ. In the New Testament, it's moving us toward Christ's return.

Promises Kept helps us see that story unfold. We will look at the Old Testament in large chunks of Scripture, rather than just one particular book. Specifically, we will look at how God is moving this story forward through covenants and events. Each covenant builds on another one, progressively revealing God's purposes in the story.

For me, it is helpful to have a visual representation of the story as well, so I've included a historical timeline of the Old Testament.[2] This gives you a framework for when and where the events and covenants occur as you are studying.

TIMELINE	SCRIPTURE REF.
CREATION	Genesis 1–2
FALL + PROMISE	Genesis 3
FLOOD (Noahic covenant)	Genesis 6
BABEL	Genesis 11
PATRIARCHS (Abraham, Isaac, Jacob)	Genesis 12–50
EXODUS + CONQUEST	Exodus–Joshua
RULE OF THE JUDGES	Judges 1–1 Samuel 9
UNITED KINGDOM (Saul, David, Solomon)	1 Samuel 10–1 Kings 11
DIVIDED KINGDOM (Judah and Israel; various kings)	1 Kings 12–2 Kings 17
EXILE	Books of Daniel, Esther, Jeremiah, Lamentations
RESTORATION	Ezra–Nehemiah

WHAT TO EXPECT FROM THIS STUDY

This study is broken up into five days using a simple Bible study method called "Observe, Interpret, and Apply."

Day 1 *Observe* the chapters for that week. My kids do a literacy program at school that asks them to "notice and wonder" about what they are reading. Observation is a foundational literacy tool. When we come to the text of Scripture (or any text), we should use what we observe, or notice, to build a foundation for our interpretation and then application.

For example: "In the beginning, God created the heavens and the earth" (Gen. 1:1). Some observations we could make are that the earth had a beginning, and that beginning started with God creating all things. Our observations of the text must always include an awareness of God within the text because He is the One who is over all things, and the One we want to know more in our study. The questions in this section will encourage you toward asking good questions of the text to uncover God's intended purpose.

Day 2 *Observe* other chapters of the Bible. (This is to supplement your study, but some weeks you will only observe the main text for that week.)

Day 3 *Interpret* the chapters for that week. Our natural inclination is to apply the text to ourselves first. We often want to ask, "What does this mean to me?" before we ask, "What did this mean in its original context?" However, we want the *interpret* section to let us understand what the text means for all time before we understand what it means for us right now.

On Day 3, we take all our observations and see how they fit together to explain the meaning of the text. I once had a teacher say, "The text can have many applications, but only one interpretation." That's what we are uncovering on this day.

Day 4 *Apply* the chapters for that week, particularly looking at where you fit in the story.

Day 5 "Where is Christ in the story?" is a short devotional with a focus on Christ's fulfillment of the Old Testament passage we have been studying that week.

To sum up, for the first three days we will be looking at the story ("What Is the Story?"). The fourth day will be application—"Where Am I in the Story?"—and the fifth day will be "Where Is Christ in the Story?" You may be wondering, *Why does the application about me come before Christ?*—and you are a good Bible student if you are asking that question! Because we are spending so much time looking at the Old Testament in this study, we are also going to spend a lot of time applying the truths of the Old Testament to our own lives. Namely, we need Jesus to come and make things right. The Bible presents us with two paths to follow: two ways to live, or two stories to find ourselves in. Only one story is the saving one—the one where Jesus is the hero.

Every day you will read the chapters for study, so by the end of the week, you will have read them at least five times. These weekly studies are designed to be done in 15–20 minutes a day, though you could always spend more time reading and studying if you wanted to!

Every week also has a key verse that you can commit to memory. I will be honest; Scripture memory is really hard for me. But I have found that the more I write the verse down or the more I listen to it on my Bible app, the easier it is for me to retain it. I am always helped when I memorize a passage of Scripture that corresponds to what I am studying or teaching. We learn in a variety of different ways, and Bible study engages every single aspect of our learning, and one of these is memorization.

If you are a Bible study leader, I have also included a Leader's Guide at the back of this study. It includes ideas and tips for leading your Bible study, suggested questions from each day of the week to ask, and suggested answers, because no one likes to go into a group study without some helps!

Whether you complete the study on your own or are preparing to lead women through it, my prayer for you as you begin this study is that you would come to wonder at the greatest story the world has ever known. It's a story worth knowing from beginning to end. It's the story of our faith.

Let's get started and start at the beginning!

THE ADAMIC COVENANT

OBSERVE THE TEXT
GOD CREATES THE WORLD

Read Genesis 1–3 each day this week before diving into the questions.

1. What is familiar to you in this text? What is new to you that you did not notice before?

2. Based on this text, what is a covenant? See the table below for the pieces of a covenant. This will help as we look at covenants throughout the following weeks.

The chart below was put together by two Bible scholars who were actually my first professors in seminary. Prior to taking their classes (Old Testament and Systematic Theology), I had never looked at the Old Testament through this lens. I did not look at it through any lens actually. But they both helped me situate myself within a cultural context in the ancient Near East during the time when the Bible was written.

Covenants and contracts were a normal part of the way of life in this time period. God comes to His creation in a way they can understand. He comes to His people in a way that is familiar to them, but then He makes it better. In the ancient Near East, the stronger party or gods could not be trusted. But God can. In His mercy, He gives them a language for understanding Him—a covenant. This helps us understand what God is doing in the covenants. He comes in the language of the ancient Near East to show them what He is like, and to bring them back to Him.

It's not necessarily easy to compare a contract with a covenant, largely because we don't typically deal in covenants today. But we do deal in contracts; think of buying a house, taking a job, and so on. A covenant has more skin in the game.[3] For one thing, there is a moral aspect to a covenant in contrast to a contract, which is more of a legal agreement. Marriage in our contemporary Western culture, for example, is often considered a legal contract, but often people will call it a covenant to emphasize the permanence of the vows taken by the two people entering into it. The chart below helps contrast the two like this:[4]

CATEGORY	CONTRACT	COVENANT
STRUCTURE: *How is it organized, and who are the parties involved?*	Transactional / list of witnesses	Speaker introduced first / blessings and curses
OCCASION: *What's the outcome of this? What's the driving force?*	Expected benefit	Desire for relationship
INITIATIVE: *Who acts first?*	Mutual agreement	Stronger party
ORIENTATION: *Who does this involve? People, or things/objects?*	Thing-oriented	Person-oriented
OBLIGATION: *What is the motivating factor?*	Performance	Loyalty

As you can see by this chart, a covenant is more personal. It is rooted in relationship—and I think we could even go so far as to say it is rooted in love. With that in view, let's dive into the first covenant.

3.   Based on these definitions, who takes the initiative in this covenant that we've just read? Who is the recipient?

4. There is a shift in Genesis 1:26 and following. What do you notice is different in these verses going forward?

5. What does God expect of humanity (vv. 28–30)?

6. What does God call His creation (v. 31)?

Scripture Memory, Genesis 1:26–28:

> *Then God said, "Let us make man in our image, after our likeness. And let them have dominion over the fish of the sea and over the birds of the heavens and over the livestock and over all the earth and over every creeping thing that creeps on the earth."*
>
> > *So God created man in his own image,*
> > *in the image of God he created him;*
> > *male and female he created them.*
>
> *And God blessed them. And God said to them, "Be fruitful and multiply and fill the earth and subdue it, and have dominion over the fish of the sea and over the birds of the heavens and over every living thing that moves on the earth."*

Let's Pray:

Lord, You are a good and gracious God who created us to bear Your image. You are the author of all creation. You fill the earth with every good thing. You spoke life into existence. Everything comes from Your good hand. We are Your creation. As we begin this study, help us to humble ourselves under Your authority over all things. In Christ's name, **Amen.**

OBSERVE THE TEXT
COVENANT EXPECTATIONS

Read Genesis 1–3.

1. God revisits His creation of humanity in Genesis 2. Look at verses 5–17.

   How does this expand what you read in Genesis 1:26–27?

   What is new here that wasn't in Genesis 1?

2. Covenants often have stipulations for obedience. What are the expectations here for Adam and Eve?

3. Sadly, the events of Genesis 3 come quickly in our Bibles after Genesis 1 and 2. Look at Genesis 3:1–7. Based on what you read in Genesis 2, what do Adam and Eve get wrong about God's commands?

4. What happens to them immediately after they eat the fruit?

5. Read Genesis 1–3 in a different version. Do you notice anything different reading it now?

Scripture Memory, Genesis 1:26–28:

Hint: This time try listening to the verses on a Bible app or read the verses out loud. Another tip for memory is to write the verses each day, then try writing from memory.

> *Then God said, "Let us make man in our image, after our likeness. And let them have dominion over the fish of the sea and over the birds of the heavens and over the livestock and over all the earth and over every creeping thing that creeps on the earth."*
>
> > *So God created man in his own image,*
> > *in the image of God he created him;*
> > *male and female he created them.*
>
> *And God blessed them. And God said to them, "Be fruitful and multiply and fill the earth and subdue it, and have dominion over the fish of the sea and over the birds of the heavens and over every living thing that moves on the earth."*

Let's Pray:

> *Lord, You are a God who is holy and perfect. You created all things good, and You expect Your created beings to follow in Your goodness. We have sinned against You time and time again. Forgive us for the ways we doubt Your good purposes in our lives. Give us renewed resolve to obey today. In Christ's name,* **Amen.**

WEEK 1 | DAY 3

INTERPRET THE TEXT
COVENANT CONSEQUENCES

Read Genesis 1–3.

1. As God's covenant people, Adam and Eve had to obey God. To be God's representatives in the world, they had to listen to what He said. They failed to keep their end of the covenant agreement. Look at Genesis 3:14–19. What are the consequences for breaking the covenant?

   What word is mentioned in verse 14 for the serpent that is not mentioned in the rest of the consequences?

2. We find two hopeful things mentioned even in the midst of the consequences.

Look at Genesis 3:15 and Genesis 3:20–21. What does God promise to do in verse 15?

In verse 20, what does Adam do?

What does God do in verse 21?

3. What do you think these promises mean?

Can you think of other places in Scripture where these promises come up again?

4. In your own words, how would you explain the consequences and promise?

Scripture Memory, Genesis 1:26–28:

Try writing Genesis 1:26–28 out from memory today.

Let's Pray:

Dear heavenly Father, You have not left us to ourselves. Thank You for giving us the hope of the promised seed. Thank You that sin was not the final word in our lives. Thank You that the penalty for our sins is not the final word in our lives. In Jesus' name, **Amen.**

APPLY THE TEXT

WHERE AM I IN THE STORY?

Read Genesis 1–3.

1. All of us are descended from one man and one woman—Adam and Eve. What does Genesis 1:26–28 say about what it means to be created by God?

2. Look up Romans 3:23 and 5:12–14. What do these verses say about the impact of Adam's sin on us?

3. Adam and Eve were created in God's image, but how did Satan distort this fact when he spoke to Eve in Genesis 3:5? How do we respond in this way too?

4. In your own words, write out where you find yourself in this story. How are you connected to Adam and Eve? How are you like them, and how have they affected you?

Scripture Memory, Genesis 1:26–28:

Fill in the blanks from memory.

> *Then God said, "Let _____ , after our likeness.*
> *And _____ over the fish of the sea and*
> *over the birds of the heavens and over the livestock and over all the earth and*
> *over every creeping thing that creeps on the earth."*
> *So _____ ,*
> *in _____ ;*
> *_____ he created them.*
> *And God blessed them. And God said to them, "_____*
> *and _____ and _____ , and*
> *have _____ over the fish of the sea and over the birds of*
> *the heavens and over every living thing that moves on the earth."*

Prayer:

Write a prayer based on how you saw yourself in this story. Maybe it is a prayer of confession, a prayer of thanksgiving for how God has saved you, or any combination of those prayers.

THE BETTER ADAM
WHERE IS CHRIST IN THE STORY?

Read Genesis 1–3.

One of my favorite modern hymns is "Come Behold the Wondrous Mystery" by Matt Boswell. In the song, Boswell writes about the first Adam and how his sin led to death. But he does not leave us there. He then points us to the One Paul calls the "second Adam." He does what the first Adam could not do. He succeeds where the first Adam failed. He is the better Adam.

We end Week 1 with bad news. Adam and Eve were created by God, placed in a perfect garden home, lived in daily fellowship with God, and had no sin. Then it all changed. When Adam and Eve chose to disobey God, paradise was lost.

God's original intent was to dwell among His people (Gen. 3:8). But God is also holy, so He cannot dwell in the presence of sinful people. Adam and Eve are cast out of the garden clouded by grief and shame. But the Bible keeps going. The story continues. Bad news is not the final news.

Within this sad ending lives a promise. Genesis 3:15 is what many scholars call the first gospel proclamation.

"I will put enmity between you [Satan] and the woman, and between your offspring and her offspring; he shall bruise your head, and you shall bruise his heel."

The New International Version packs an even more potent punch: "He [Eve's offspring] will crush your head, and you will strike his heel."

At first glance, Satan has won. He convinced Adam and Eve that following their own path was preferable to following God's. Their sinful choices led to tragic consequences for themselves and all who came after them. The world was never to be the same.

But God is rich in mercy.

Three hopeful things emerge from this encounter.

First, God promises to deal with sin through the offspring of the woman. Adam responds in faith that God will do what He says. Satan might grasp at the heel of the offspring of the woman—and he will inflict damage. But ultimately the offspring of the woman will prevail. He will crush the enemy's head once and for all.

Next, Adam responds in faith in Genesis 3:20 when he names his wife Eve, "the mother of all living." God said her offspring would crush the head of the serpent, and Adam gives her a name that signifies he believes God.

Then, God clothes them with animal skins (Gen. 3:21). You see, they suddenly realized they were naked (a symbol of their shame over their sin), and God takes decisive action to cover their nakedness by the death of another living thing.

In all this, God the Creator acts on their behalf. He will not leave His created beings to their own destructive devices. He cares too much. He loves too much. He's invested so much.

> We respond in faith, believing that what God says He will accomplish, He will do.

This "offspring" will come. But He's not just any offspring. He's the very Son of God (John 20:31). You see, it takes more than just a human to deal with the problem of sin. The Redeemer had to be human, but He also had to be perfect. Adam was our representative as the first human. But he also was our representative as a sinner. Just look at what Paul says about Adam and Christ in 1 Corinthians 15:21–28:

For as by a man came death, by a man has come also the resurrection of the dead. For as in Adam all die, so also in Christ shall all be made alive. But each in his own order: Christ the firstfruits, then at his coming those who belong to Christ. Then comes the end, when he delivers the kingdom to God the Father after destroying every rule and every authority and power. For he must reign until he has put all his enemies under his feet. The last enemy to be destroyed is death. For "God has put all things in subjection under his feet." But when it says, "all things are put in subjection," it is plain that he is excepted who put all things in subjection under him. When all things are subjected to him, then the Son himself will also be subjected to him who put all things in subjection under him, that God may be all in all.

The covering that God provided for Adam and Eve as they fled the garden was a foretaste of the covering all who trust in Jesus Christ receive by His perfect record in our place. The work Christ accomplished on the cross is the "head-crushing" work needed to bring us back into fellowship with God. Like Adam, we respond in faith, believing that what God says He will accomplish, He will do.

Christ is the perfect and better Adam. He is the Man who followed God's Word without fail. He is the God-man who can deal with our sin once and for all. The story ends with tragedy, but hope breaks through. Redemption is on the horizon.

Reflection:

How is Christ the better Adam? What does He do that Adam failed to do, and where in Scripture do you see this play out?

Scripture Memory, Genesis 1:26–28:

If possible, write out the entire passage for this week: Genesis 1:26–28.

Let's Pray:

Dear Lord, what hope we have in Christ! You have not left us alone in our sin but sent Christ to do what Adam failed to do. You have not condemned us to die, but redeemed us by the second Adam's perfect obedience, sacrifice, and resurrection to new life. Give us continued faith to trust in Your good purposes that You have come to redeem what was lost. You will not leave Your creation in their sin. You have come to us and will come again. In Christ's name we pray, **Amen.**

THE ABRAHAMIC COVENANT

Another covenant—the covenant with Noah in Genesis 6–9—comes between this next one and the previous one we studied. For the purposes of this study, we will work through the major covenants and events that move the one overarching redemptive narrative forward. The covenant with Noah reveals God's character and purposes in the world, but it is not included in this study for the sake of time and for working within the framework of the metanarrative.

Let's Review:

The story of Scripture is a progressive one. God's Word is living and active (Heb. 4:12), which means you can always grow from reading it. But it is also designed to be read in context. As we have learned, God moves His story forward through covenants and events, so each week we are going to look back to get our bearings. The goal of this study, and any study of Scripture, is greater biblical literacy. In reviewing what we have learned we build that literacy muscle. Sometimes the review will be a paragraph overview of what you learned the day before, and sometimes it will be a full overview calling you to remember where you are, but hopefully by the end of this study you will have a good grasp of the Old Testament covenants and how Christ fulfills them.

We are only one week into this study, so we do not have a lot to review. But remember what you learned about God last week? He created all things and called His creation good. He asked His first created beings, Adam and Eve, to obey Him, to be fruitful and multiply, and to rule over the world He made. They lived in unbroken fellowship for a time with their Creator. But then sin entered the world through their distrust and disobedience, breaking the fellowship and plunging all of creation into rebellion and decay. Thus began the long journey back to being in fellowship with God in a fully redeemed home. That is where we start this week.

OBSERVE THE TEXT

GOD MAKES A PEOPLE

*Read Genesis 12, 15, and 17 each day this week
before diving into the questions.*

1. Remember the pieces of a covenant that we learned about last week? How do
    you see these pieces at play with Abraham and God in Genesis 12, 15, and 17?
    Look back at the chart in Week 1 Day 1 if necessary.

2. What is promised in this covenant? Remember that it's a progressive covenant,
    so you'll need to look at all three chapters to see what's promised.

3. What seems to be the problem with these promises? For a hint, look at Genesis 15:2.

4. Look back at Genesis 15. Who is the acting agent in this covenant?

   What is Abraham's role?

   What does this tell you about God and how He is working in the story of Scripture?

5. Read Genesis 12, 15, and 17 in a different version. What new things do you learn?

How does reading these chapters in a different version expand your understanding? What words are different, and how does the different wording bring greater clarity for you?

Scripture Memory, Genesis 12:1–3:

Now the LORD said to Abram, "Go from your country and your kindred and your father's house to the land that I will show you. And I will make of you a great nation, and I will bless you and make your name great, so that you will be a blessing. I will bless those who bless you, and him who dishonors you I will curse, and in you all the families of the earth shall be blessed."

Let's Pray:

Lord, You are on a mission to make a new family and undo all that was lost in Adam. Thank You for calling Abraham out of darkness to walk in your light. Thank You that we are part of his family and blessed by his offspring. In Christ's name, **Amen.**

OBSERVE THE TEXT

COVENANT PROMISES

Read Genesis 12, 15, and 17.

1. In Genesis 17, God expands on the covenant. Look at verses 1–8. What does God do for Abraham, and what does He ask Abraham to do in verses 9–14?

2. We are told Abraham's age in Genesis 12 and then again in Genesis 17. For how many years did Abraham live with the promise?

3. Notice verses 17–18 in chapter 17. Where does this come from? Who is he talking about? Use your cross references in your Bible to identify what he is talking about. Genesis 16 will also be helpful. Why is this an important detail?

4. God restates the promises of the covenant in Genesis 17:1–8. How is it expanded or further explained?

5. What attributes of God are displayed in these three chapters?

Scripture Memory, Genesis 12:1–3:

Try listening to these verses in a Bible app this day, and then practice writing the verse to reinforce memorizing.

> *Now the LORD said to Abram, "Go from your country and your kindred and your father's house to the land that I will show you. And I will make of you a great nation, and I will bless you and make your name great, so that you will be a blessing. I will bless those who bless you, and him who dishonors you I will curse, and in you all the families of the earth shall be blessed."*

Let's Pray:

Lord, You play the long game with Your people. Your concept of time is not like my concept of time. Thank You that You don't ever stop working in the lives of Your people, even when it does not always feel like You are working. In Christ's name, **Amen.**

INTERPRET THE TEXT

COVENANT HOPE

Read Genesis 12, 15, and 17.

1. Look up Matthew 1. What is traced in verses 1–17?

   How is this covenant promise fulfilled in this genealogy of Jesus?

2. Think about Genesis 17. God changes Abram's name to Abraham and has him circumcise himself and his household. What do you think these things say about what God expects for Abraham and his descendants?

3. Briefly skim Genesis 49–50. How is this promise to Abraham beginning to see fulfillment? What do these chapters say about their expectation of these promises?

4. Can you paraphrase this covenant or write it in your own words?

   How would you explain this covenant to a new person coming to your Bible study?

Scripture Memory, Genesis 12:1–3:

Try listening to the verse in a Bible app this day, and then practice writing the verse to reinforce memorizing.

> *Now the* Lord *said to Abram, "Go from your country and your kindred and your father's house to the _____ that I will show you. And I will _____ ___ ____ __ _____ _____, and I will _____ _____ and make your _____ _____, so that you will be a blessing. I will bless those who bless you, and him who dishonors you I will curse, and ___ _____ ____ ____ _____ __ ___ _____ _____ __ _____."*

Let's pray:

> *Lord, You are a God who blesses Your people with gifts we don't even think to pray for. Thank You for upholding Your promises to Your people. Thank You for working over the course of our lives to keep Your promises. Give us eyes to see how You are working in the world, even when we can't see Your promises coming to pass. In Jesus' name,* **Amen.**

APPLY THE TEXT

WHERE AM I IN THE STORY?

Read Genesis 12, 15, and 17.

1. Read Luke 1:46–55 and 67–79. What do these songs from Mary and Zechariah say about the promise to Abraham and to our place in this promise?

2. Read Colossians 3:1–14 in the New International Version. How is what God calls you to in this passage similar to what God calls Abraham to in Genesis 17?

3. What had Abraham done (referred to in Gen. 17:17–18) that made him circumvent the process? See Genesis 16 to get the full story.

How are you tempted to go outside of God's covenant promises to you when He seems slow?

4. Remember the genealogy in Matthew. Read Revelation 21:1–3 too. If you're not a direct descendant of Abraham, how is this covenant fulfilled in your life?

Scripture Memory, Genesis 12:1–3:

Practice writing the verses from memory today. You could also place a piece of paper over the verse as you write. Only look if you really cannot remember.

Let's Pray:

Lord, I am tempted to go outside Your covenant when You seem slow to me. Please help me trust You even when I can't see Your hand working in the details of my life. Help me remember where I am in the covenant story (a spiritual descendant of Abraham) when it feels like Your promises are slow. In Jesus' name, **Amen.**

BUILDING THE FAMILY

WHERE IS CHRIST IN THE STORY?

Read Genesis 12, 15, and 17.

How many of us can trace our family trees back for hundreds, let alone thousands, of years? I know the names of my great-grandparents, but beyond that I'm a little lost. I have some general history and know some locations of birthplaces, but my genealogy stops at the turn of the twentieth century at best.

This is not true with the descendants of Jonathan and Sarah Edwards. Over 1,300 descendants can trace their roots back to this godly couple years after they both passed away in 1758. Their legacy includes people who became doctors, lawyers, politicians, and other sorts of influential leaders.

Abraham has a few centuries on them.

In Matthew's genealogy, Abraham's lineage is traced from him all the way to Jesus Christ. At the start of the New Testament, this is significant. Abraham was specifically promised that from one man (him), all the families of the earth—that is, all nations—would be blessed (Gen. 12:1–4). At the end of Matthew, Jesus tells His disciples to go and make disciples of *all nations* (Matt. 28:18–20). From Jesus Christ comes one new people: the people of God. Abraham's covenant promises begin small. He only has one son who is the child of the covenant. He dies with one son who carries that covenant forward, a tiny plot of land, and a promise. Though—thousands of years later—through that one offspring salvation is offered to all.[5]

One could read this promise as "through Isaac—the offspring—all the nations are blessed." And that would not be wrong. He is the promised son. But it's also more than that. Isaac begins the process of a long line of "promised offspring" that pave the way for the true and better offspring to come and bless all nations once and for all. Abraham, Isaac, and Jacob could not provide the blessing that we all need. Like every person who came before them and after them, they died. Like every person who came before them and after them, they sinned. Like every person who came before them and after them, they needed to be saved from their sinful nature as much as anyone does.

But Jesus Christ, the long-awaited Son of Abraham? Death couldn't hold Him. He never sinned. And He is able to save all who put their faith and trust in Him.

> The promised offspring has come to build God's family and take them home to glory.

In Him, we truly are blessed. The covenant with Abraham promises two very important things—land and offspring. This is important because, remember, God's people were always intended to be His people, in His place, under His rule. God's heart is to bring His people back to what He intended for them. In Abraham's offspring, He's doing just that. He's making a people for Himself from every tribe, tongue, and nation. He's making a home for us where death and sin have no place. In Christ, this promise is fulfilled right now, and will be finally completed one day. The promised descendant has come and one day He will take us home to His land forever.

This is why He came. He dwelt among us to bring us back to God's place, to live as His people, under His loving rule. So when Jesus looks at His disciples on the night before His death and says "in my Father's house are many rooms" (John 14:2–6), this covenant finds its fulfillment. The promised offspring has come to build God's family and take them home to glory.

Reflection:

Do you feel "homesick" for this future home? If you don't, spend some time praying that God would give you an eternal perspective of longing for this future home.

Scripture Memory, Genesis 12:1–3:

Fill in the blanks:

Now _____, "Go from your country and your kindred and your father's house _____. And I will make of you _____, and I will _____ and make your name great, so that you will be a blessing. I will _____ _____, and him who _____ you I will curse, and in you _____."

THE MOSAIC COVENANT

Let's Review:

Welcome to Week 3! In this progressive story, we have gone from God creating the world and everything in it to those created people (Adam and Eve) rebelling against Him, leading to sin entering the world. In Genesis 3:15, God gives a promise that from Eve an offspring would come. This offspring would once and for all deal with the curse brought into the world through sin.

From then on, we watch the woman and the seed. This is why it is so striking that Abraham is chosen by God. His wife, Sarah, is barren (Gen. 11:30), so how could the offspring come from her? Here's the answer: But God. He is in the business of doing impossible things. So He does what only He can do—He opens Sarah's womb, gives the couple a child, and with that child comes the promise: he will be a blessing to all the nations.

God created His people (Adam and Eve), put them in His place (Eden), and dwelt among them. The covenant with Abraham starts the family over with a new line and a continued promise: the offspring of the woman will not only crush the head of the serpent, but He will be the means of bringing God's people back into right relationship with Him.

But God's people have a problem. When we find them this week they have just come out of slavery in Egypt (more on that in Week 6), and they have not a clue how to live in "His place under His rule."

Let's look at the Mosaic covenant.

OBSERVE THE TEXT
COVENANT PEOPLE

Read Exodus 19–20:17; Exodus 24 each day this week
before diving into the questions.

1. What questions do you have as you read? What new things stand out to you? What is familiar to you? Did you find repeated words or phrases? Circle or underline them as you read.

2. In the beginning of this section, Moses sets the context of this covenant. What had happened before this point? Where have they come from and what had God done for them? (You may need to flip back to Exodus 14 to understand the full context.)

How recently had this happened?

3. Look at Exodus 19:4–8. What does God do in this covenant? What is expected of His people, those He had brought out of Egypt? What do the people promise to do?

4. Now look at Exodus 20:1–17. Some have divided the Ten Commandments into categories. What categories do you find, and which commandments fit under each?

5. In Exodus 24, the people receive the Lord's words from Moses. What does Moses do to establish this covenant with the people (see vv. 5–8)?

Scripture Memory, Leviticus 20:26:

> *"You shall be holy to me, for I the LORD am holy and have separated you from the peoples, that you should be mine."*

Let's Pray:

Lord, You are holy. You are righteous. You are good. You have called us to be holy as You are holy. But we have sinned against You, and on our own we would be unable to stand in Your presence. Yet, You have given Your Son to come to us and save us. You have made us holy and called us to You. Thank You for showing Your holiness to us in the face of Jesus Christ and by His grace letting us live. In Christ's name, **Amen.**

OBSERVE THE TEXT
COVENANT LIVING

Read Exodus 19–20:17; Exodus 24.

1. Think back to the previous covenants we have studied. What has already been promised to God's people? What is God preparing His people for in the Mosaic covenant?

2. In Exodus 19:10–24, God gives Moses instructions for the people and the priests. Make a list of all that is involved. Why do you think He has them do these things before they receive His Law?

3. What do these Ten Commandments teach the Israelites about God? How do they direct their relationships with their neighbors and the land they are about to possess?

4. Read Exodus 19–20:17 and 24 in a different translation. What new things do you learn? What words are different in this translation, and how do the differences give greater meaning to the text?

Scripture Memory, Leviticus 20:26:

Try listening to the verse on a Bible app and writing down the verse as you hear it. This helps reinforce memory. Another trick with listening to verses is to listen while you do something else (like clean, drive, or even exercise).

> *"You shall be holy to me, for I the LORD am holy and have separated you from the peoples, that you should be mine."*

Let's Pray:

> *God, when we look at Your commandments, we see Your compassion and Your holiness. We see Your justice and Your mercy. You care about Your creation, Your people, and our relationships. Thank You for revealing Yourself to us through Your law, helping us see how holy and merciful You are. In Christ's name,* **Amen.**

INTERPRET THE TEXT
WHAT DOES IT MEAN?

Read Exodus 19–20:17; Exodus 24.

1. Look up the word "consecrate" in a dictionary. What does the word mean? What does it say about God and His relationship with His people, the Hebrews, that He has them do this?

2. How will they fulfill their end of the covenant? What is the significance of blood in this covenant?

3. In Exodus 24:15–18, God's presence descends on the mountain in the form of a consuming cloud. How many days did the cloud cover the mountain, and on what day did God speak to Moses? Does it sound like something you've read before in this study? How does this event move the story forward as you think about what God is doing in the overarching narrative of Scripture?

4. Can you paraphrase this covenant? If so, write it down. How could you explain this covenant to your neighbor or friend who doesn't know Christ?

Scripture Memory, Leviticus 20:26:

Tip: Put a piece of paper over the verse and practice writing from memory.

"You shall be holy to me, for I the LORD am holy and have separated you from the peoples, that you should be mine."

Let's Pray:

Lord, You call us to come to You in humility and in awareness of our sinfulness. We cannot stand in Your presence, but You still come to us and make a way. Thank You for not leaving us to ourselves and for providing us a way to know You, to know Your expectations, and to know how desperately we need a Savior. In Christ's name, **Amen.**

LAW VS. GRACE
WHERE AM I IN THE STORY?

Read Exodus 19–20:17; Exodus 24.

1. Look over the Ten Commandments again in Exodus 20:1–17. Are there any you can say you have kept perfectly?

2. Look at Exodus 24:3. What does this commandment mean to you? Can you think of a time when you had this sort of resolve to obey? What happened? How long did it last?

3. How do you react when you read these laws and requirements?

4. Read Hebrews 8–9. How does this encourage you knowing that you live on this side of the Mosaic covenant?

5. Imagine you are talking about the Ten Commandments with an unbelieving friend. How would you explain their purpose and what our response to them should be?

Scripture Memory, Leviticus 20:26:

Write the verse out two or three times.

"You shall be holy to me, for I the LORD am holy and have separated you from the peoples, that you should be mine."

Let's Pray:

Dear heavenly Father, we are so thankful to stand on the other side of the Mosaic covenant. Christ is better and has fully completed the law and its demands. Over and over again we have resolved to obey and fallen short. But Christ obeyed perfectly. And we get all His righteousness in our place. Thank You for revealing our need so we can see our great Savior. In Christ's name, **Amen.**

DO WE NEED THE LAW NOW?
WHERE IS CHRIST IN THE STORY?

We have reached the place in our study where many people give up on their Bible reading, and you've made it this far—congratulations! You have made it through the Mosaic covenant.

When I graduated from college, the president of the school instructed families to hold their applause until the end of the ceremony. As I walked up to the stage I looked to the back of the auditorium and saw my three younger brothers poised to stand up. They looked like they were ready to cheer for their favorite team in the Super Bowl, while I was ready to crawl into a hole. As I walked across the stage, the sound of their cheers and applause made it seem as though the entire room was celebrating my graduation. The college president had a hard time containing his laughter as he handed me my diploma, knowing that the effort to keep three rowdy teenage boys quiet was a futile one. Afterward, my dad leaned over and said, with a smirk on his face, "There are some who follow the rules, and some who ask for forgiveness later."

He's not wrong. Two types of people in the world are those who follow rules and those who see rules as "suggestions." I imagine you know which one you are the most often. But if you've ever spent time trying to obey all the rules set before you, I imagine you know how hard it is. We're all a little (or a lot) rebellious sometimes.

The New City Catechism sums up the Mosaic covenant—otherwise known as the law—perfectly.

Question: Since no one can keep the law, what is its purpose?

Answer: That we may know the holy nature of our God, and thus our need for a Savior.[6]

Do you feel the exhaustion in the Mosaic covenant? Do you get to the end of it and wonder, *Then who can be saved?* It's hard to read the Mosaic law and not feel the weight of God's holiness and our inability to measure up. There's just so much blood. There's so much expectation. There's so much requirement.

That's the point.

And if you are at the point of the study where you feel a little defeated, you are on the right track. Remember, this is a progressive story, meaning each part goes together. Each covenant reveals another aspect of God's divine plan in saving a people for Himself, of restoring His people to His place under His rule.

As God's people leave Egypt and wander about in the desert, they need to know how to live in the land they are about to possess. After hundreds of years waiting for the Abrahamic covenant to be fulfilled, they are now ready to receive their portion. But they have been living as slaves in a foreign land. Now they are about to be God's people in His place. As former slaves under pagan kings, they do not know what godly living looks like. So, they need boundaries. They need expectations. They can't just dwell in God's presence and live as they always have.

Something—someone—needs to stand in their place. Someone has to ready them to enter His presence.

The Mosaic covenant pulls back the curtain even more and makes a way for God's people to live in His presence. But it was never complete. There was a perpetual need for cleansing because "it is impossible for the blood of bulls and goats to take away sins" (Heb. 10:4 NIV).

Every time they slaughtered an animal for their sin, they felt the weight of the continual need for redemption. Every time they failed to keep their end of the covenant, they felt the weight of the lack of completion. It had to be done over and over and over again just so they could maintain a right relationship with God. But as we will see throughout the rest of this study, even this was never enough.

They needed a perfect substitute.

In John 1:29, John the Baptist cries out, "Behold, the Lamb of God who takes away the sin of the world!" In every aspect of His earthly ministry, Jesus was preparing Himself to be the sacrifice they (and we) need to remove the stain of sin and lead people into obedience.

> The law was never meant to crush us. It was meant to lift our gaze and stir our longings for the Messiah who could keep the law perfectly.

What does Jesus say on the cross? "It is finished" (John 19:30).

What does Hebrews say He does after making purification for sins? He sat down (Heb. 1:1–4).

What the law could not do, Jesus did once and for all (Rom. 8:3–4). If we only had the Mosaic covenant, we would be crushed under its expectations. But it was never meant to crush us. It was meant to lift our gaze and stir our longings for the Messiah who could keep the law perfectly.

As we said above, two types of people are law-keepers and law-benders. But the Bible tells us they are the same. The ones who think they keep the law are fooling themselves. The ones who don't even try are killing themselves.

Instead, Jesus kept it for us. We stand condemned under the Mosaic covenant, ever in need of a substitute. Jesus Christ is that substitute. In Him, we stand forgiven and free to walk in obedience. The law-keeper and the law-bender meet and find hope at the foot of the cross.

Reflection:

Are you tempted toward being a law-keeper, or a law-bender? How does Christ's obedience to the Mosaic covenant convict or encourage you?

Scripture Memory, Leviticus 20:26:

Fill in the blanks:

"You shall _____ to me, for I _____
and have _____, that you should be mine."

Let's Pray:

Lord, we thank You that today we stand forgiven if we are trusting in Christ. His perfect record is our perfect record. Help us believe that no amount of law-breaking or law-keeping will save us or condemn us. He has paid it all. **Amen.**

THE DAVIDIC COVENANT

OBSERVE THE TEXT

THE KING AND HIS KINGDOM

Let's Review:

We are now past the halfway point! Congratulations! We have looked at God's covenant with Adam and how that played out: God kept His word, Adam didn't. We have looked at God's covenant with Abraham and how that played out: God gave Abraham a child and a promise to bless the nations through that son. We have looked at God's covenant with this new family, the nation of Israel, as God prepared His people to enter the land by giving them His rules to live by.

In every instance, God is working to bring His people back. Remember, He created the world and everything in it and called it good. He wants to dwell among His people, in His land, with them living joyfully under His rule. But time and again, the people fail to live up to their end of the deal. God is faithful—they are not. Sound similar to your own life? I know it does mine.

So now we have God's people living in God's land—but there is just one missing link. They don't have a king. With that we turn to the Davidic covenant.

*Read 2 Samuel 7:1–17; Psalm 89:1–4 each day this week
before diving into the questions.*

1. Do you notice any repeated words or phrases? If so, underline or highlight those.

2. What are the parts of this covenant? Who is the acting agent? Who is God making this covenant with?

3. What are the expectations of this covenant for both parties?

4. How is this covenant similar to or different from the previous covenants we have looked at?

5. What do we know about this king? (Look ahead to 2 Samuel 11.)

Scripture Memory, Psalm 89:3–4:

> *"I have made a covenant with my chosen one;*
> *I have sworn to David my servant:*
> *'I will establish your offspring forever,*
> *and build your throne for all generations.'"*

Let's Pray:

> *Lord, You are a good king. You are a gracious king. Your kingdom knows no end, and Your righteousness extends to all generations. There is no kingdom that is not under Your complete power and control. You make kings rise and fall. Thank You for showing your goodness and kindness to us in King Jesus, the one to whom all kings will one day bow. In Christ's name,* **Amen.**

OBSERVE THE TEXT
THE REALITY OF THE KING

Read 2 Samuel 7:1–17; Psalm 89:1–4.

1. Let's look at the context. This covenant comes in a specific time in Israel's history. Look at Judges 21:25, Ruth 1:1, and Ruth 4:13–22. What do you notice about these texts in relation to what is happening in 2 Samuel 7?

2. Now let's see what God says about the king. Look up Deuteronomy 17:14–22. What did God expect from the king? How does David compare to these expectations?

3. But David is not the first king Israel had. Look up 1 Samuel 8:1–9. What is displeasing to Samuel with the elders' request for a king to be appointed over their nation?

What do you know about the outcome of their first king, Saul? (Saul started out well enough, but later was disobedient. You can read about his downfall in 1 Samuel 13:9–14 and 1 Samuel 15, and how God dealt with him in 1 Samuel 16:14.)

4. Read 2 Samuel 7:1–17 and Psalm 89:1–4 in a different translation. How is your understanding of this covenant expanded by reading it in these passages? What word or phrase differences help illuminate the text for you?

Scripture Memory, Psalm 89:3–4:

Listen to Scripture on the Bible app and practice writing it out as you listen. This helps reinforce memory. You could also try writing out the verses in your own words—as a paraphrase.

> *"I have made a covenant with my chosen one;*
> *I have sworn to David my servant:*
> *'I will establish your offspring forever,*
> *and build your throne for all generations.'"*

Let's Pray:

> *Lord, we are surrounded by kings who do everything that is right in their own eyes. They do not bow to You. They do not submit to You. They do not honor You. We admit that we often look to kings like the nations, and not like You desire for Your people. Give us faith to trust and desire the king of Your choosing and not our own. In Christ's name,* **Amen.**

INTERPRET THE TEXT
WHAT DOES ALL THIS MEAN?

Read 2 Samuel 7:1–17; Psalm 89:1–4.

1. Read 2 Chronicles 6:1–11 and 1 Kings 11:1–8 together. What is going wrong in the progression of the story of Scripture?

2. In 1 Kings 15:1–8, we are given the reason that God keeps the line of David going. What is it?

3. The people wait a long time for a better king to come. Read Matthew 1:1–17. After reading this genealogy, what have you learned about why God preserved the line of David?

4. Is there an attribute of God that stood out to you in the beginning of this day's text in 2 Samuel 7 or Psalm 89? What is it, and how does it help explain the covenant and God's purposes in the world?

5. Can you paraphrase the covenant with David? Write it out in your own words.

Scripture Memory, Psalm 89:3–4:

Try writing out the verses multiple times. Each time you write, try looking at the verses less than you did before.

> *"I have made a covenant with my chosen one;*
> *I have sworn to David my servant:*
> *'I will establish your offspring forever,*
> *and build your throne for all generations.'"*

Let's Pray:

Dear heavenly Father, You are faithful to Your end of the covenant. When we fail, You are faithful. When we do not keep our end of the deal, You deal kindly and graciously with us. Your ability to keep Your word is not determined by our ability to keep ours. Thank You that You kept working to keep Your promise to David so we could be part of this story—part of this line of salvation that is filled with equally sinful people who need a Savior. You have established Your covenant forever. Thank You for this gift. In Christ's name, **Amen.**

APPLY THE TEXT
WHERE AM I IN THE STORY?

Read 2 Samuel 7:1–17; Psalm 89:1–4.

1. After reading all the expectations God had for those who would rule as king over Israel (Deut. 17:14–22) and seeing how it actually played out, do you think it was ever possible for any king to perfectly follow his end of the covenant?

2. We all long for a good king or leader. How have your expectations of a king or a kingdom been met or disappointed in your life?

3. Read Psalm 2. Who is the true King promised here? Which king are you serving: the king "like the nations" or the true King? What does serving Him look like in your life?

Scripture Memory, Psalm 89:3–4:

Put a piece of paper over the verses and try reciting them from memory. If you struggle, try listening to it on a Bible app again as you recite it.

> *"I have made a covenant with my chosen one;*
> *I have sworn to David my servant:*
> *'I will establish your offspring forever,*
> *and build your throne for all generations.'"*

Let's Pray:

Dear Lord, the nations rage against You, but You are on Your throne. When we are discouraged by kings who fail to measure up, help us to trust Your goodness. No king will be enough, but the perfect King is always enough. Help us humble ourselves before Your mighty hand, knowing that You will one day deal with all the kings who rage against You. Help us trust You when we are defeated and overwhelmed by the brokenness of earthly leaders. Lift our gaze to Your throne and Your perfect rule and reign. In Christ's name, **Amen.**

THE TRUE AND BETTER KING

WHERE IS CHRIST IN THE STORY?

I've woken up super early for three weddings, but only was a participant in one of them. Like millions of people all over the world, I set my alarm for the royal weddings of both Prince William and his younger brother, Harry. As an American looking from the outside in, I am enchanted by the pomp of the monarchy. Maybe if I actually lived close to it, its fascination would fade and I would not be as intrigued. But because I am not bound by a monarchy, I can get caught up in the idealism and trappings of it all.

Whether we live under a monarchy or not, we are often interested in royalty. Why? Deep in our hearts we long for a king. Even if you did not set your alarm ridiculously early to watch two people you didn't know get married, you probably want to live under a benevolent ruler. You want to live in a world where righteousness and justice reign. You want a king or leader who will look out for your best interests, and the interests of all who are under his care. The problem is we rarely get all those things. Like Israel before us, we are left longing for a better king. We create one of our own making and then are disappointed when he fails us.

When Israel finally got a king, hope was in the air. After the disappointment with Saul, David had all the marks of a great king. He loved God. He led the people to love God. He even wrote many of the psalms in the book of Psalms.

But he also was an adulterer and a murderer. Some have even called him a rapist, since as the king, he was in a position of power over Bathsheba. Though he repented of his sin poignantly, as recorded in Psalm 51, he was not the king God was looking for to rule His people. They needed a perfect king.

Then Solomon came along, and in many ways, he was even better than his father. No one surpassed him in wisdom (1 Kings 4:30). Israel finally had prosperity and was a blessing to the nations (1 Kings 10). But we can't omit the sad part of his personality and actions: his love for idol-worshiping women. He lived well in his youth only to end his life with a divided heart.

> Jesus might not have been the king they expected, but He is the King they, and we, so desperately need.

Time after time, Israel was let down by a king who was not enough to lead the people to wholehearted obedience to God. These kings were a hard reminder that even *mostly* devoted is not enough to remove the stain of sin. The people needed a king who was completely devoted to God, His law, and His purposes for His people.

We can run through the history of every leader of Israel and review the lives of all the well-known characters in the Bible. But we'd find that even the best and brightest and wisest of them could not measure up to Jesus. He's the only perfect man who ever lived.

When Jesus comes on the scene in Matthew 1, hope bursts anew. Matthew knows what he is talking about when he links Jesus directly to the line of Abraham and David. He is reminding his audience—those of a Jewish background—of what they should know: that there is a covenant waiting to be fulfilled. In the Abrahamic covenant, God promises the land and the offspring. In the Mosaic covenant, God promises a people who will live under His law. In the Davidic covenant, God promises that the King will come and establish His rule and reign.

And in Matthew 1, He's here. But He wasn't the king they expected, one who would restore Israel politically. He was not a king like other nations had ruling over them—confined to a specific time and place—but He was the King who drew all the nations to Himself (Matt. 8:5–13). He was not a king who ruled by might, but He was the King who ruled by love (John 13). He was not a king who disobeyed; He was the King who obeyed perfectly all the way to death (Phil. 2).

In every instance of the kingdom coming, Jesus might not have been the king they expected, but He is the King they, and we, so desperately need.

Let the words of Isaiah 9:6–7 wash over you:

> *For to us a child is born,*
> *to us a son is given;*
> *and the government shall be upon his shoulder,*
> *and his name shall be called*
> *Wonderful Counselor, Mighty God,*
> *Everlasting Father, Prince of Peace.*
> *Of the increase of his government and of peace*
> *there will be no end,*
> *on the throne of David and over his kingdom,*
> *to establish it and to uphold it*
> *with justice and with righteousness*
> *from this time forth and forevermore.*
> *The zeal of the LORD of hosts will do this.*

Behold, our King!

Reflection:

Some have said that Jesus' kingdom is an "upside-down kingdom." What does this mean to you?

Scripture Memory, Psalm 89:3–4:

Fill in the blanks from memory:

"I have _____ with my _____;
I have sworn to _____:
'I will establish your _____,
and build your_____.'"

Let's Pray:

Lord, Your kingdom is an upside-down kingdom. We are often confronted with a kingdom we don't expect or understand. Your ways are not our ways. Your thoughts are not our thoughts. When we are confronted with a kingdom that does not make sense, give us eyes to see Your work in the world. Your kingdom knows no end. You will rule and reign over all things. You are the better and perfect King. **Amen.**

THE NEW COVENANT

OBSERVE THE TEXT

GOD'S DOING SOMETHING NEW

Let's Review:

In this progressive revelation of God's purposes in the world, we have looked at His very good beginning in creation. We have seen the devastation sin brought into the world. Then we learned of the hopeful beginnings of a new family in Abraham, and the promise that the whole world would be blessed through His offspring.

After four hundred years of slavery in Egypt, God's people were led out by Moses and brought into a new land. (If you would like to learn about how Israel ended up in Egypt, read Genesis 46.) It was in this land that God established His people as a nation, a nation with laws that would govern them civically, morally, and ceremonially. If they followed His ways, they and the land would be blessed, and the nation would be a blessing to other nations as a testimony to God.

In every instance, we hope, "Maybe this time they will be able to live under God's rule perfectly." But even in the land, the law was not enough. We don't talk about the time of the judges much in this study, but even a quick glance at the book of Judges reminds us that God's people could not obey without strong leadership. They could not possess the land and dwell securely without help.

Could a king help the citizens of Israel be faithful to God's law? That's the million-dollar question, right? But you have come this far in the study, and you know that even a strong king is not enough. The king is human, meaning he, too, falls short of God's commands and God's perfection. The Davidic covenant establishes the kingship, but we know enough about the Davidic line to know that King David does not measure up. He fails too. Miserably.

So where do we turn? We move forward in this story and find that in every instance, human efforts fail the people. God continues to work in the world He has made, even as His people flounder. God continues to give them promises, glimpses, and hope for restoration. But it has become abundantly clear that something better is needed. The time for external fixes is over—God's people need something new.

So we turn to the new covenant.

Read Jeremiah 31 each day this week before diving into the questions.

1. What repeated words or phrases do you notice in this text? Write them down.

2. Look at verses 31–34. What are the parts of this covenant?

3. Who is receiving this covenant? Who is the acting party in this covenant? Count how many times God uses a personal pronoun ("I" or "me").

4. What does this covenant promise? Make a list of everything you notice.

5. Does this covenant promise anything new that you have not read in this study before?

Scripture Memory, Jeremiah 31:33:

Read over the memory verse multiple times. Write it out two or three times to begin cementing it in your mind.

> *"For this is the covenant that I will make with the house of Israel after those days, declares the LORD: I will put my law within them, and I will write it on their hearts. And I will be their God, and they shall be my people."*

Let's Pray:

Lord, we have felt the weight of our sin. We know our inability to keep Your law and follow Your commands. We know our inability to do what You have asked of us. We know that we need a transformation from the inside out. Thank You for the promise of this new covenant that makes a way for us to be right with You. In Jesus' name, **Amen.**

OBSERVE THE TEXT
A BRIEF HISTORY LESSON

Read Jeremiah 31.

1. What is Jeremiah calling God's people back to in this chapter? (Look up Jeremiah 11:10 for a hint.)

2. Read Deuteronomy 30:17–20 and write down the warning God gives Israel.

Now write His promise.

3. The prophetic books happen concurrently with the historical books. They are the prophetic response to Israel's experience. Read 2 Chronicles 36 and write down the fulfillment and the context of Jeremiah's time period. What kings of Judah are mentioned? What other nation is mentioned? What is happening here in this text? (You may be confused by the Israel/Judah distinction. As told about in the historical books, after Solomon's death the nation of Israel split into two kingdoms. Subsequent rulers of the southern kingdom, Judah, were descended from David and Solomon. Israel became the northern kingdom, whose rulers descended from a host of other tribes of Israel. The promised off-spring is now traced through Judah after the nation splits into two kingdoms. But "Judah" and "Israel" can be used interchangeably to mean the nation of God's people.)

4. Summarize the state of God's people when Jeremiah gives them the promise of a new covenant.

5. Read Jeremiah 31 in a different translation. What do you notice that is similar? What do you notice that is different?

6. What attribute of God shines most brightly in this text?

Scripture Memory, Jeremiah 31:33:

Try listening to this verse multiple times on a Bible app. Recite it out loud as you listen.

> *"For this is the covenant that I will make with the house of Israel after those days, declares the LORD: I will put my law within them, and I will write it on their hearts. And I will be their God, and they shall be my people."*

Let's Pray:

Lord, You come to us in our rebellion and shame and make a way for us to be right with You. You write Your law on our hearts. You turn hearts of stone into hearts of flesh. Instead of running from us in our sin, You run to us to bring us back to You. Thank You for the amazing truth that our rebellion is not the last word. In Christ's name, **Amen.**

INTERPRET THE TEXT

A NEW HOPE DAWNS

Read Jeremiah 31.

1. How did every covenant we've studied up to this point move the story of Scripture forward? (This is a challenge to remember all you've been learning!) What elements of this new covenant are similar to the previous covenants?

2. Read Ezekiel 36:24–29. How does the new covenant tie all these covenants together?

3. What went wrong with the covenant that God made when He took the people out of Egypt (Jer. 31:32)?

4. This covenant turns the old covenants on their head. Every other covenant had stipulations for the nation of Israel. This one does not. Look up Luke 22:14–23. How does this passage explain why this promise to, as Jeremiah 31:34 puts it, "remember their sin no more" is possible?

5. Can you paraphrase this covenant or explain it in your own words? Imagine you are telling it to a friend who is unfamiliar with the Old Testament.

Scripture Memory, Jeremiah 31:33:

Using a piece of paper to cover the verse, write the verse out from memory.

> *"For this is the covenant that I will make with the house of Israel after those days, declares the LORD: I will put my law within them, and I will write it on their hearts. And I will be their God, and they shall be my people."*

Let's Pray:

Lord, You are our God. What an amazing truth! You no longer count our sins against us. What an amazing truth! The chasm between us and You has been closed because of Christ's shed blood. Thank You for the new covenant that makes a way for us to be right with You. In Christ's name, **Amen.**

APPLY THE TEXT
WHERE AM I IN THE STORY?

Read Jeremiah 31.

1. In Jeremiah 31:31, Jeremiah says that God is making a new covenant with the houses of Israel and Judah. If you are not part of those houses—and many of us aren't!—how is this covenant true for you? Look up Ephesians 2:11–3:6 for help explaining this concept.

2. Is there a sin in your life—maybe something in the past or something you currently struggle with—that seems too impossible to be forgiven? Write down Jeremiah 31:34 and replace "their iniquity" and "their sin" with that specific sin. Pray that God would give you faith to believe this to be true for you.

3. Jeremiah continues this promise of a new covenant in Jeremiah 32:37–41. Read this passage and ask yourself how you have been a recipient of God doing good to you. Write down your thoughts.

4. Imagine you are talking with an unbelieving friend or neighbor who feels the weight of her own sin. How does this covenant help her understand God's purposes? How does this tie in with the gospel message of the New Testament?

Scripture Memory, Jeremiah 31:33:

"For this is the covenant that I will make with the house of Israel after those days, declares the LORD: I will put my law within them, and I will write it on their hearts. And I will be their God, and they shall be my people."

Let's Pray:

Dear heavenly Father, there is nothing in us that we bring to the table to earn our salvation. But You have made a way for all people of all nations to be brought to You in addition to the Israelites You first called! Thank You for bringing anyone who comes to You into Your family by the blood of Christ. **Amen.**

KEEPING COVENANT FOR COVENANT BREAKERS

WHERE IS CHRIST IN THE STORY?

If you knew the meal you were eating tonight was your last, what would you choose? I know what I'd pick. Always tacos. My choice of a last meal reveals just how human I am. Given moments to live, I think of my own hunger pains.

On the flip side, when His moments to live on earth were numbered, Jesus thinks about His followers—and all who came before, and all who will come after.

In His final moments alive, Jesus shares a meal with His friends. Every gospel writer chooses a different angle to take on these events. But all of them focus on something important—everything is about to change. John writes about the coming Holy Spirit (John 14–17). Matthew, Mark, and Luke write about the institution of the Lord's Supper and the removal of our sins by the blood of Jesus (Matt. 26:17–35; Mark 14:12–26; Luke 22:14–23).

All this is the fulfillment of the new covenant promised in Jeremiah 31. Jeremiah in effect tells Israel, "There is coming a day when your hearts will be transformed." God promises to again dwell among His people. He promises to forgive and forget all the wrongs they have committed against Him.

But there is one big obstacle standing in their way—their sin. As we have reiterated throughout this study, you know that no amount of effort on any person's part will make him or her obey. Our good intentions fail miserably. Every single time. This is why the final words of Jesus to His disciples are such a comfort to them and to us.

In Luke 22:20, He explains that this blood of the new covenant is a symbol of His blood that He will shed for them. This would have triggered a significant memory in their minds. Every year, and even that week, they would prepare a lamb for slaughter. This Passover ritual had gone on for centuries. And it still had to be repeated the next year and the year after that and so on. It was never enough. But in the new covenant promise of Jeremiah 31, there is an echo of permanency. This new covenant is not written on tablets of stone, but it's written on human hearts (2 Cor. 3:3). This new covenant contains the promise of sins being cast as far as the east is from the west (Ps. 103:12; Jer. 31:34).

> Every single covenant in the Old Testament was driving home the reality that we were always going to need a new heart.

The only one who could do this is God Himself.

Even when the promise of the new covenant came in Jeremiah 31, God's people could not maintain their end of the bargain. When they entered the land back in the time of the Mosaic covenant, God warned them that they would lose the promised land if they disobeyed Him. Over a long period of time, they disobey Him over and over again. As we learned, after King Solomon's death, the nation of Israel splits into two kingdoms—north and south (Israel and Judah). Both nations are taken into exile because of their disobedience. The Assyrians take Israel. Babylon takes Judah.

After seventy years, the exiles do return from Babylon as we read about in Ezra and Nehemiah, but the people's obedience is short-lived. And then four hundred years of silence falls upon them . . . until a certain baby is born and hope springs anew. This baby is the promised seed of Genesis 3:15. The firstborn of creation. He's the offspring of Abraham, who blesses the nations by His very existence. He obeys the law perfectly, not only in the letter of the law, but in His spirit too. He's from the line of David ruling as the better King. He's the fulfillment of the new covenant, securing our redemption by His own blood.

Often we hear people make a distinction between the old and new covenants. The Old Testament is left behind, but the New Testament is where it's at. But if we look closely at Jesus Christ, we see there is no distinction. There is no old covenant; there is just a broken covenant, which is why the new is even necessary. From the very beginning, God's people have broken covenant with Him. Every single covenant in the Old Testament was driving home the reality that they were always going to need a new heart—one they could not create on their own.

This is where the new covenant leads us—the culmination of every promise in the Old Testament, kept by our Savior in the new. That's what we've been doing in this study. We have flexed our Bible muscles to help us bear the weight of what the Old Testament has been telling us all along, that every story whispers His name.[7]

Reflection:

How does the promise that His blood takes away sin change how you interact with unbelievers who feel weighed down by their own sin? How does this promise encourage believers?

Scripture Memory, Jeremiah 31:33:

Fill in the blanks:

> *"For this is _____ that I will make with _____ after those days, declares the* LORD: *I will _____, and I will _____. And I will be _____, and they shall be _____."*

Let's Pray:

> *Lord, when we are weighed down with our sin, help us remember this truth and this hope. You have given us new hearts. You have cleansed us by Your blood. You have changed our old nature and given us a new nature in Christ. We praise You for the finished work of Christ, the One who secured the new covenant by His own life, death, and resurrection.* **Amen.**

THE PASSOVER *and the* EXODUS

OBSERVE THE TEXT
GOD PROTECTS HIS PEOPLE

Let's Review:

Whenever I get to the end of a study, I feel a little sad. I've spent so much time immersed in a text of Scripture, I find that the people have become familiar friends. Especially when I am doing the study in community with other believers, the shared experience learning from God's Word together is something I want to savor.

I actually hope you find yourself with the same low-level sadness! You are now in the sixth week of your study. You have worked your way through five covenants in the Old Testament. That is no small task! Many people rush through the Old to get to the New. But you stayed with it and have learned a lot. Well done!

Covenants are not the only way God moves the story forward in the Old Testament. He also moves the story forward with events. For the sake of time, we are going to look at a significant event reiterated often throughout Scripture—the Passover coupled with the exodus. We are examining this last because it is tied closely to the Mosaic covenant but also informs the other covenants going forward. You have that framework of God's intention to bring His people back to His place under His rule, and with new hearts in view. Once you get to the end of this week, you will see that the building blocks for the new covenant—and ultimately the cross—began a long, long time ago.

Let's go back to Egypt.

Read Exodus 12:1–13, 29–42; 14:13–31.

This week's setup will be slightly different since it is not following a covenant, so the days will be broken into two parts, the Passover and the exodus, as you'll see.

The Passover: Exodus 12:1–13, 29–42

1. What do you read that is familiar? What do you read that is new?

2. Try reading in a different translation and see if you notice anything new.

3. Read Exodus 11:4–7 for context. What is God commanding Israel to do here, and why? Write down the process as you observe it in this text.

4. What does God promise the people (and nation) of Israel if they obey Him? What is the basis for that promise coming true?

The Exodus: Exodus 14:13–31

1. What do you read that is familiar? What do you read that is new?

2. Pick a different translation to read from and see if it adds to what is new or familiar to you.

3. What is happening in this scene? What is Israel's response to what is happening?

4. What does God do for Israel in this scene? What does God do to the Egyptians?

Scripture Memory, Deuteronomy 5:6:

"I am the LORD your God, who brought you out of the land of Egypt, out of the house of slavery."

Let's Pray:

Lord, You are the God who delivers Your people. There is no army or nation or person that is too strong to overcome Your people. You deliver us from bondage to sin. You deliver us from suffering. You are the same God today that You were back then. You are unchanging. **Amen.**

OBSERVE THE TEXT

THERE IS ONLY ONE GOD

Read Exodus 12:1–13, 29–42; 14:13–31.

The Passover: Exodus 12:1–13, 29–42

1. Skim Exodus, chapters 7–10. What is happening in these plagues and in this time of Israel's history?

2. Taking all the plagues together, what do you learn about how Israel is delivered from the Egyptians and the plagues they face?

3. If you could pick one word to describe God in this text, what would it be?

The Exodus: Exodus 14:13–31

1. How long does this entire event take? (Notice the references to time and night and day.)

2. Look at verses 18 and 25b. Write down what the verses say the Egyptians will learn about God.

3. Look at verse 31. Write down what has resulted from the events described.

4. What does this passage teach you about God?

Scripture Memory, Deuteronomy 5:6:

Listen to the Scripture in a Bible app multiple times today. Try practicing the verse as you listen.

"I am the LORD your God, who brought you out of the land of Egypt, out of the house of slavery."

Prayer:

Write out a prayer today based on what you learned about God in the passage you studied. Let it be your prayer of worship and adoration to Him.

INTERPRET THE TEXT
WHAT DOES THE STORY MEAN?

Read Exodus 12:1–13, 29–42; 14:13–31.

The Passover: Exodus 12:1–13, 29–42

1. This event defined Israel's history, and even still does to this day. God commanded Israel to remember this event every year (Lev. 23:1–5; Num. 9:1–5; Deut. 16:1–6). Why do you think it was so important for the people to remember this event?

2. What does that tell you about how God saves His people? Why is it so important that God saves His people in this way?

3. In your Bible, look up any additional cross references (if you don't have a Bible with cross references, a study Bible or Bible app should have them). How do the additional passages help you understand this text?

The Exodus: Exodus 14:13–31

1. Look back at the verses you wrote down on Day 2. What is God saying about Himself in the story of the exodus?

2. Read Hebrews 11:27–29. How does the author of Hebrews explain how God's people were delivered? What was the difference between them and the Egyptians? What is the similarity between us and them?

3. How do these two events connect to the other covenants and help you understand God's purposes in moving the story forward in this way?

Can you paraphrase Exodus 12:1–13, 29–42, and Exodus 14:13–31? How would you explain it to a classroom of elementary school students?

Scripture Memory, Deuteronomy 5:6:

Write the passage down multiple times today. Each time you write it, try doing it from memory more than the previous time.

"I am the LORD your God, who brought you out of the land of Egypt, out of the house of slavery."

Let's Pray:

Lord, You deliver us in the same way today. We are saved by Your power and Your power alone. We are saved by Your blood alone. We are saved by Your grace alone. We are saved by Your work alone. You have always been about saving Your people from helpless situations in ways that only You can. Help us trust You when it seems like You aren't working, knowing that You still work in the lives of Your people even today—saving by the blood of the perfect Passover Lamb. **Amen.**

APPLY THE TEXT
WHERE AM I IN THE STORY?

Read Exodus 12:1–13, 29–42; 14:13–31.

1. Read 1 John 5:1–8. What action words are present? What does this mean for your life? How is your life connected to the "water, blood, and Spirit"?

2. Think about the two ordinances given to the church: baptism and the Lord's Supper. How does your participation in these connect you to the exodus and Passover?

3. In Isaiah 43:2, God says to Israel that when they "pass through the waters, I will be with you." Can you think of a time in your life when you were frightened, when you were passing through dark waters and God was with you? Did that experience strengthen your faith? How?

4. Let's tie it all together. See if you can write down from memory every covenant and event we have studied together (there are only six, remember!) and how God worked in moving the story forward through those covenants and events.

Scripture Memory, Deuteronomy 5:6:

Put a piece of paper over the verse and try writing the verse straight from memory. Then say it out loud from memory.

> *"I am the LORD your God, who brought you out of the land of Egypt, out of the house of slavery."*

Let's Pray:

> *Lord, there is no sin we experience that You are not fully sufficient to make a way through. Thank You for the blood of Jesus that covers us. Thank You that Jesus passed through the waters for us, so we only get life. Thank You for the promise that You are with us in every situation we face because our sin no longer condemns us. In Christ's name,* **Amen.**

WHERE IS CHRIST IN THE STORY?

Read Exodus 12:1–13, 29–42; 14:13–31.

Have you ever gotten through something harrowing by the skin of your teeth? I went through a decade of medical crises that often confounded doctors. I've had high-risk pregnancies, multiple surgeries, and at the end of that long decade, I had a hysterectomy to remove cancer that had remained hidden for nearly eighteen years. There are times I look at my life and think, *I shouldn't be here, except for the grace of God.*

All of life is a gift, but for the most part we live without contemplating this reality. If we are healthy or crisis-free, we forget that death is often a heartbeat away from us. The fact that we live is reason to celebrate. We have been delivered from death, often without even knowing it. That's how I imagine these scenes in Exodus 12 and 14. God gives the Hebrews the command, death hovers at their door, and then they are given little notice to eat their protective meal and make a mad dash out of Egypt. This was not a meal to savor. It was a meal to cover them and then get them out the door. And then when they cross the Red Sea, it was not an easy process. With walls of water on either side of them, they make the long trek across to safety—with Egyptians closing in behind.

It's no wonder this event carried them all throughout their journey in the wilderness, into the promised land, and beyond. This was their definitive marker of God's deliverance. They could not get out of slavery on their own. They could not resist the death angel alone. They could not cross the Red Sea on their own.

God provided every step of the way. So, every year they remembered this moment where they were delivered through blood and water. The Passover is mentioned over seventy times in the Bible. The majority of those times are in the Old Testament, and when it is mentioned in the New Testament it is either as a historical marker or as Christ as the Passover Lamb. Jesus ate the Passover with His disciples on the night before He died, and then He told them about the new covenant (which we looked at in Week 5). He's our Passover Lamb (1 Cor. 5:7). The blood of a lamb at Passover had to be spilled again and again each year. But Christ's blood was spilled once, and that is enough for all time.

Their deliverance from death both through blood (the lamb) and water (crossing the Red Sea) is a symbol for our own deliverance. His blood covers us, and the waters of judgment can't touch us. When we repent of our sins, trust in Christ, and obey Him in baptism, we tell this story. We are covered by the blood and raised to walk in newness of life. We have crossed to the other side safely because Christ paid the price and went before us both in death and in life.

Every step of the way, we are carried by another. Every step of the way, Israel was too. But for us, that act of redemption has already been accomplished and is enough to make us fully clean and fully redeemed.

As in every other part of this story of Scripture, God is telling His people, "It's always been by My hand that you're saved." We might feel like we're getting in by the skin of our teeth, but He is the acting agent every time. He creates us. He calls us. He redeems us. And He will carry us all the way home.

Reflection:

How has your understanding of the one story of Scripture been expanded these last six weeks?

Scripture Memory, Deuteronomy 5:6:

Fill in the blanks from memory:

"I am the _____, who brought you out of _____, out of the _____."

Prayer:

Write a prayer of praise at the conclusion of this study thanking God for the ways He has worked in your life.

A STORY WORTH TELLING

I have always loved the Old Testament. True confession: my undergraduate degree is in English, so I gravitate toward narrative, poetry, and digging into context and history. The Old Testament is filled with images and stories that force us to use those tools we learned in our high school English classes—and I love it.

But I get it—some people find the Old Testament difficult. We are so far removed from the Old Testament time period that sometimes we don't understand what is happening. Generally speaking, we deal in legal contracts rather than covenants, which usually have a moral or personal component, so we might miss the significance of the covenants God made with His people.

With thirty-nine books, the Old Testament is longer than the New, which has twenty-seven; but often we spend more time in the New Testament. It feels easier to understand. It contains the stories of Jesus and the hope of the gospel. But without the Old Testament we can never make complete sense of the New. Jesus quotes the Old Testament. The apostles quote the Old Testament. It was their only Scripture. Most importantly, Jesus Christ fulfills the Old Testament. Without a clear understanding of the importance of the events of the Old Testament, much of the New Testament will be lost on us. We will be reading Scripture in black and white when the Bible as a whole is intended to be viewed in technicolor.

Just consider John the Baptist's words in John 1:29 when he says, "Behold, the Lamb of God, who takes away the sin of the world!" What if we didn't understand the significance of "the lamb"? Then it would seem so strange to us that Jesus is *the* Lamb, right? But in that context, the people hearing him knew exactly what John was saying—the Messiah has come.

The book of Romans is full of allusions to the Old Testament—every covenant actually. But if we don't understand those covenants, when Paul brings up Abraham or the law or David or the new covenant, we only understand in bits and pieces. The Bible was meant to be understood in full.

So I hope by the end of this study you have tasted God's goodness in the Old Testament and that you have a greater desire to feast further on His Word. This is only a sampling—an appetizer really—there is so much more to enjoy and discover. But this is not just a feast for you to enjoy for yourself. We are called to feast on God's Word and then invite other people to the banquet.

When God's Word gets ahold of you, you should want to share it with others (Matt. 28:18–20). If you have benefited from taking in the Scriptures these last six weeks, my prayer for you is that this won't be the end of your journey. Let it be the beginning, and then bring others along with you. If you have been a participant in the study, maybe your next step is to invite a friend to do the study with you or even lead a small group. If you have been a leader of the study, maybe your next step is to train up another leader to launch a new group. Let the Word of Christ dwell in you richly, and then let it spread like wildfire among God's people.

Welcome to the beginning. I pray you continue on this journey of discovering God's glory in all of the Scriptures.

LEADER'S GUIDE

A NOTE TO BIBLE STUDY TEACHERS:

First, let me say that you are doing good work. It is no small thing to research curriculum, plan a study, and prepare yourself to lead women to study God's Word together. Well done! I'm honored you chose this study.

I have been a Bible study leader, and I know how hard it is to come to a study and not know where to begin. There are a number of ways to use this one. The most straightforward way is to ask your women to do each week's lessons before coming to discuss. If your study is discussion-based (particularly in a small group setting), this Leader's Guide will help you know which questions to ask to best lead a study. All those questions will come from the homework that week.

If you are leading a larger group Bible study, you may want to spend more time teaching. But first, ask every woman to do her homework. The study will only be as fruitful as the time the participants put into it. Your students need to know this. They will learn and grow by first handling the text themselves, then coming to the study for reinforcement of what they have learned. Once they have done this, you can gather together to teach the text as a commentary to what they have studied.

Whether you are doing a small group study only or adding in small groups before or after teacher time, there are struggles in leading a group through a study. Every study group has a person in the group who loves the study and loves to talk about what she has learned. I've been this person on numerous occasions! But we also know there are women in our groups who have helpful things to say but need a little coaxing. In the small group time, try asking someone directly if they would answer a question. You could also let them know in advance that week before that you plan to ask them the question. Not everyone enjoys being put on the spot without time to think about the question! Small group time is a perfect time to identify new leaders and teachers. Pay attention to the ones who seem most talkative, most engaged with their demeanor, and even the one who seems to have written down a lot during the homework time. These might be your next leaders. Asking people in advance to share what they learned that week gives you a controlled environment to test a woman's gifts to lead, and also encourages greater participation in the group.

The study of God's Word is best done in community, so these questions are designed to lead women to own the text for themselves, but also to discuss with others. A Bible study environment should encourage both of these outcomes. Even if your study is larger, I have included some suggested smaller group questions in the Leader's Guide to facilitate the discussion.

I am praying for you as you prepare. You are embarking on a wonderful task—taking women to the feast of God's Word. You will not be disappointed.

The following are suggested questions. Feel free to pull from other questions in the study as you lead. You know your group best.

LEADER'S GUIDE

WEEK ONE: THE ADAMIC COVENANT

Suggested Questions:

Some of these questions could be discussed in a smaller group (groups of 2–4), and some can be handled in a larger group (groups of 5–15). I have included suggestions next to the questions that would be especially pertinent for smaller groups, though of course you can also use them for any size group.

Opener: Have you ever signed a contract? For what? Have you ever been involved in a broken agreement? Have you ever made a covenant? What was involved?

1. Look at the chart in Week 1 Day 1:

   Based on these definitions, who takes the initiative in this covenant we just read? Who is the recipient?

2. What does God expect of humanity (Gen. 1:28–30)?

3. God revisits His creation of humanity in Genesis 2. Look at verses 5–17. How does this expound on what you read in Genesis 1:26–27? What is new here that wasn't in Genesis 1?

4. Sadly, the events of Genesis 3 come quickly in our Bibles after Genesis 1–2 (though we cannot know how much real time actually went by). Look at Genesis 3:1–7. Based on what you read in Genesis 2, what do they get wrong about God's commands?

5. We find two hopeful things mentioned even in the midst of the consequences. Look at Genesis 3:15 and Genesis 3:20–21. What does God promise to do in verse 15? What does Adam do in verses 20–21? What does God do?

6. **Smaller Group:** Look up Romans 3:23 and 5:12–14. What do these verses say about the impact of Adam's sin on us?

7. Adam and Eve were created in God's image, but how did Satan distort this fact when speaking to Eve in Genesis 3:4–5? How do we respond in this way too?

8. **Smaller Group:** When you wrote out in your own words where you find yourself in this story, what did you say? How are you connected to Adam and Eve? How are you like them and how are you affected by them?

9. How is Christ the better Adam? What does He do that Adam failed to do, and where in Scripture do you see this play out?

10. Practice your memory verse as a group.

WEEK TWO: THE ABRAHAMIC COVENANT

Opener: Have you ever felt homesick? What made you feel that way? What did you long for?

1. Do you remember the pieces of a covenant that we learned about last week? What are they? How do you see these pieces at play with Abraham and God in Genesis 12, 15, and 17? (Look back at the chart if necessary.)

2. What is promised in this covenant? Remember that it's a progressive covenant, so you'll need to look at all three chapters to see what's promised.

3. In Genesis 17, God expands on the covenant. Look at verses 1–8. What does God do for Abraham, and what does He ask Abraham to do in verses 9–14?

4. We are told Abraham's age in Genesis 12 and then again in Genesis 17. For how many years did Abraham live with the promise?

5. **Smaller Group:** Notice verses 17–18 (Gen. 17). Where does this come from? Who is he talking about? Use the cross references in your Bible to identify what he is talking about. Genesis 16 will also be helpful. Why is this an important detail?

(Note to Leaders: You could come to your group time with this information ready and then have the members look up the references in small group time.)

6. Look up Matthew 1. What is traced in verses 1–17? How is this covenant promise fulfilled in this genealogy of Jesus? Read Revelation 21:1–3 too. If you're not a direct descendant of Abraham, how is this covenant fulfilled in your life?

7. **Smaller Group:** Read Luke 1:46–55 and 67–79. How do these songs from Mary and Zechariah speak to Abraham's promise and our place in this promise?

8. Read Colossians 3:1–14 out loud in the NIV. Compare what God is calling you to in this passage to what God calls Abraham to in Genesis 17.

9. What did Abraham do in this story (Gen. 17:17–18) that made him circumvent the process? How are you tempted to go outside of God's covenant promises to you when He is slow?

10. Practice your memory verse as a group.

WEEK THREE: THE MOSAIC COVENANT

Opener: Can you think of a time where you viewed rules as a "suggestion" rather than a rule? How do you feel when you break a rule? Why do you feel this way?

1. Look at verses 19:4–8. What does God do in this covenant? What is expected of them? What do they promise to do?

2. **Smaller Group:** Now look at Exodus 20:1–17. What categories do you find in the Ten Commandments? Which commandments fit under each?

3. In Exodus 24, the people receive the Lord's words from Moses. What does Moses do to establish this covenant with the people (see vv. 5–8)?

4. In Exodus 19:10–24, God gives Moses instructions for the people and the priests. Make a list of all that is involved. Why do you think He has them do these things before they receive His law?

5. What do these Ten Commandments teach the people about God? about their relationships with their neighbors and with the land they are about to possess?

6. Read Exodus 24:15–18 out loud. God's presence descends on the mountain in the form of a consuming cloud. How many days did the cloud cover the mountain, and on what day did God speak to Moses? Does it sound like something you've read before in this study? How does it move the story forward as you think about what God is doing in the overarching narrative of Scripture?

7. **Smaller Group:** Look over the Ten Commandments again in Exodus 20:1–17. Are there any you can say you have kept perfectly?

8. Look at Exodus 24:3. What does it say? Can you think of a time when you had this sort of resolve to obey? What happened? How long did it last?

9. How do you feel when you read these laws and requirements?

10. **Smaller Group:** Skim Hebrews 8–9. How do these chapters encourage you, knowing that you live on this side of the Mosaic covenant?

11. Practice your memory verse as a group.

WEEK FOUR: THE DAVIDIC COVENANT

Opener: What qualities do we look for in a king or leader today? How does the reality that Jesus' kingdom is an "upside-down kingdom" transform that?

1. What are the expectations of this covenant for both parties?

2. How is this covenant similar to or different from the previous covenants we have looked at?

3. What do we know about this king? (Look ahead to 2 Samuel 11.)

4. **Smaller Group:** Let's look at the context. This covenant comes in a specific time in Israel's history. Look at Judges 21:25, Ruth 1:1, and Ruth 4:13–22. What do you notice about these texts in relation to what is happening in 2 Samuel 7?

5. Now let's see what God says about the king. Look up Deuteronomy 17:14–22. What did God expect from the king? How is David different from or similar to these expectations?

6. **Smaller Group:** Read 2 Chronicles 6:1–11 and 1 Kings 11:1–8 together. What is going wrong in the progression of the story of Scripture?

7. The people wait a long time for a better king to come. Read Matthew 1:1–17 out loud. After reading this genealogy, what have you learned about why God preserved the line of David?

8. **Smaller Group:** We all long for a good king or leader. How have your expectations of a king or a kingdom been met or disappointed in your life?

9. Read Psalm 2 out loud. Who is the true King promised here? Which king are you serving: the king "like the nations" or the true King? What does serving Him look like in your life?

10. Practice your memory verse as a group.

WEEK FIVE: THE NEW COVENANT

Opener: What has been your experience with the Lord's Supper, or Communion? How does your church observe it? What does the Lord's Supper have to do with the new covenant? How would you explain its significance to someone who either isn't a believer or who is merely going through the motions of a religious ritual?

1. What does this covenant promise? Make a list of everything you notice.

2. Does this covenant promise anything new that you have not read in this study before?

3. What is Jeremiah calling God's people back to in this chapter? (Look up Jeremiah 11:10 for a hint.)

4. Read Deuteronomy 30:17–20 out loud and explain the promise and warning God gives Israel.

5. **Smaller Group:** Look up 2 Chronicles 36 and summarize the state of God's people when Jeremiah gives them the promise of a new covenant.

6. Ask someone to prepare in advance to answer this question or make it a "popcorn" answer time where each person answers one part of the story. How did every covenant up to this point move the story of Scripture forward? (This is a challenge to remember all you've learned up to this point!) What elements of this new covenant are similar to the previous covenants?

7. Read Ezekiel 36:24–29. How does the new covenant tie all these other covenants together? What went wrong with the covenant that God made when He took the Hebrews out of Egypt (Jer. 31:32)?

8. This covenant turns the old covenants on their head. Every other covenant had stipulations for Israel. This one does not. Look up Luke 22:14–23. How does this explain why this promise in Jeremiah 31:34 to "remember their sin no more" is possible?

9. In Jeremiah 31:31, Jeremiah says that He is making a new covenant with the houses of Israel and Judah. If you are not part of those houses—and many of us aren't!—how is this covenant true for you? (Look up Ephesians 2:11–3:6 for help explaining this concept.)

10. **Smaller Group:** Jeremiah continues this promise of a new covenant in Jeremiah 32:37–41. Read this passage out loud and ask your group how you have been a recipient of God doing good to you.

11. Practice your memory verse as a group.

WEEK SIX: THE PASSOVER AND THE EXODUS

Opener: How has your understanding of the one story of Scripture been expanded these last six weeks?

1. Read Exodus 11:4–7 for context. What is God commanding Israel to do here and why? Write down the process as you observe it in this text.

2. Look at Exodus 14:13–31. What is happening in this scene? What is Israel's response to what is happening?

3. This event defined Israel's history, and even still does to this day. God commanded Israel to remember this event every year (Lev. 23:1–5; Num. 9:1–5; Deut. 16:1–6). Why do you think it was so important for them to remember this event?

4. What does that tell you about how God saves His people? Why is it so important that God saves His people in this way?

5. **Smaller Group:** Read Hebrews 11:27–29 out loud. How does the author of Hebrews explain how God's people were delivered? What was the difference between them and the Egyptians? What is the similarity between us and them?

6. **Smaller Group:** Read 1 John 5:1–8 out loud. What action words are present? What does this mean for your life? How is your life connected to the "water, blood, and Spirit"?

7. Think about the two ordinances given to the church: baptism and the Lord's Supper. How does your participation in these connect you to the exodus and Passover?

(Note to Leaders: For further reading on baptism and the Lord's Supper, read Romans 6:1–11, Matthew 26:27–28, 1 Corinthians 11:24–25. In these Scripture readings, write down the connection between what God is doing in the deliverance of the Israelites and what He does in our deliverance from sin. What is their memorial for remembering His deliverance? What is ours?)

8. In Isaiah 43:2, God says to Israel that when they "pass through the waters, I will be with you." Can you think of a time in your life when you passed through dark and scary waters and God was with you? How did that strengthen your faith?

9. **Smaller Group:** Let's tie it all together. See if you can recite every covenant and event from memory (there are only six, remember!) and how God worked in moving the story forward through those covenants and events. Turn to the person next to you and do it together!

10. Practice your memory verse as a group.

BIBLE MEMORY VERSES REVIEW

WEEK 1

Then God said, "Let us make man in our image, after our likeness. And let them have dominion over the fish of the sea and over the birds of the heavens and over the livestock and over all the earth and over every creeping thing that creeps on the earth."

So God created man in his own image,
in the image of God he created him;
male and female he created them.

And God blessed them. And God said to them, "Be fruitful and multiply and fill the earth and subdue it, and have dominion over the fish of the sea and over the birds of the heavens and over every living thing that moves on the earth."
(Genesis 1:26–28)

WEEK 2

Now the LORD said to Abram, "Go from your country and your kindred and your father's house to the land that I will show you. And I will make of you a great nation, and I will bless you and make your name great, so that you will be a blessing. I will bless those who bless you, and him who dishonors you I will curse, and in you all the families of the earth shall be blessed." **(Genesis 12:1–3)**

"You shall be holy to me, for I the LORD *am holy and have separated you from the peoples, that you should be mine."* **(Leviticus 20:26)**

"I have made a covenant with my chosen one;
   I have sworn to David my servant:
'I will establish your offspring forever,
   and build your throne for all generations.'" **(Psalm 89:3–4)**

"For this is the covenant that I will make with the house of Israel after those days, declares the LORD: *I will put my law within them, and I will write it on their hearts. And I will be their God, and they shall be my people."* **(Jeremiah 31:33)**

"I am the LORD *your God, who brought you out of the land of Egypt, out of the house of slavery."* **(Deuteronomy 5:6)**

FOR FURTHER STUDY

D. A. Carson, *The God Who Is There: Finding Your Place in God's Story* (Grand Rapids: Baker Books, 2010).

Edmund P. Clowney, *The Unfolding Mystery: Discovering Christ in the Old Testament* (Phillipsburg, NJ: P&R Publishing, 2013).

Peter J. Gentry and Stephen J. Wellum, *Kingdom through Covenant* (Wheaton, IL: Crossway, 2012).

Graeme Goldsworthy, *According to Plan: The Unfolding Revelation of God in the Bible* (Downers Grove, IL: InterVarsity Press, 2002).

Trent Hunter and Stephen Wellum, *Christ from Beginning to End: How the Full Story of Scripture Reveals the Full Glory of Christ* (Grand Rapids: Zondervan, 2018).

Vaughan Roberts, *God's Big Picture: Tracing the Storyline of the Bible* (Downers Grove, IL: IVP Books, 2003).

ACKNOWLEDGMENTS

Of all the things I write, these are the words that stress me out the most. It takes so many people to make a book or study possible. But here is my feeble effort to acknowledge the people who played a part in bringing this study to completion.

A study on the covenants and Christ's fulfillment of them is only possible because of the theological training I have received. I'm forever thankful for my time at the Southern Baptist Theological Seminary. Dr. Peter Gentry and Dr. Stephen Wellum transformed my understanding of how to read the New Testament in light of the Old. Dr. Brian Vickers taught me how to interpret the Bible in his hermeneutics class. I often go back to lessons learned during those years.

I still remember what it felt like to lead my first Bible study in my home. I joke that Jen Wilkin is the reason I get myself into these situations because she continues to tell me this is possible. Here I am again, with her encouragement in my ears. Thank you, Jen, for believing that I could (and should) teach the Bible. Thank you for creating pathways for women like me to teach other women to love God with their mind.

Trillia Newbell has been a faithful friend and cheerleader. This time is no different. Thank you, friend, for continuing to believe I have something to write and contribute.

The entire team at Moody has been so gracious throughout this process. Thank you, Judy, Pam, and so many others, for bearing with this novice Bible study author.

Don Gates is a good friend and wise agent. Thank you for continuing to bear with me, Don. Your wisdom and expertise make my job as a writer so much easier.

Most of my days are spent in the trenches of local life in Little Rock. I couldn't do writing without the faithful support of my church family—Immanuel Baptist Church. My pastor, Steven Smith, encourages me to use my gifts in writing and teaching. Thank you, Dr. Smith, for leading us with humility and pouring God's Word into us weekly. If I write anything of value, it's because you've been so faithful to shepherd us in the Word. The staff I serve with at Immanuel was a constant dose of encouragement as I labored over this project—thank you, friends! It's a joy to do ministry with you.

With every project, my family is as much a part of it as I am. My boys (Luke, Zach, Seth, and Ben) offered prayers and encouragement. They rejoiced when Mommy was done too! Thank you, boys, for cheering me on! My husband, Daniel, is a constant support throughout the many early mornings and late nights of trying to bring this project to completion. There is no one I would want to do this crazy life with besides you, babe. Thank you for believing that God has gifted me for this task, and for making space for me to do it.

What a gift it is to write about our Savior and His perfect plan throughout all the Scriptures. In the days when it feels like God has stopped working, I would stop and remember that He is the same. He keeps His promises. All glory goes to Him.

NOTES

1. Theologian and author Graeme Goldsworthy developed this framework to describe God's kingdom. *The Big Picture Story Bible* by David Helm (Wheaton, IL: Crossway Books, 2014) is written for children and follows this pattern to explain the continuous story of the Bible.

2. Adapted from D. A. Carson, ed., *NIV Zondervan Study Bible* (Grand Rapids: Zondervan, 2015), xxvi–xxxi.

3. "What Is the Difference between a Covenant and a Contract?," Got Questions, updated January 4, 2022, https://www.gotquestions.org/difference-covenant-contract.html.

4. Adapted from Peter J. Gentry and Stephen J. Wellum, *Kingdom through Covenant: A Biblical-Theological Understanding of the Covenants* (Wheaton, IL: Crossway, 2018), 172.

5. It is important to emphasize that though Abraham had other sons (Gen. 25:1–2), only Isaac is the child of the covenant God made with Abraham. His son with Hagar, Ishmael, is frequently mentioned in Scripture, and God promised to make a great nation through him also (Gen. 21:11–13). But the line to Christ goes through Isaac, as the promised offspring to Abraham and Sarah, so Isaac is the covenantal child.

6. "Question 15," *New City Catechism* (Wheaton, IL: Crossway Books, 2017), http://newcitycatechism.com/new-city-catechism/#15.

7. Sally Lloyd-Jones, *The Jesus Storybook Bible: Every Story Whispers His Name* (Grand Rapids: Zonderkidz, 2007).

"The book of Isaiah is where my
new-believer mind and grieving-mom heart
grasped onto the hope offered by God."

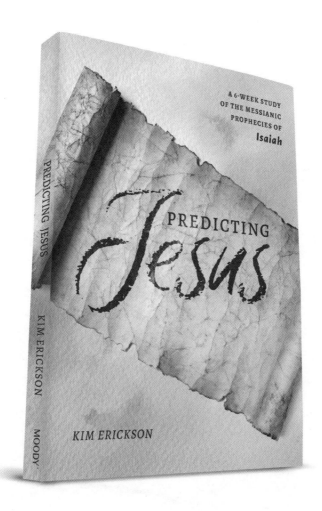

**MOODY
Publishers**

From the Word to Life

After losing her small child, the book of Isaiah became
Kim's rock of faith. She needed *proof* that God was real and
assurance that He would come through on His promises.
Join Kim on a rich, soul-strengthening study of the great
prophet who pointed the way to *Predicting Jesus*.

978-0-8024-2511-9 | also available as an eBook

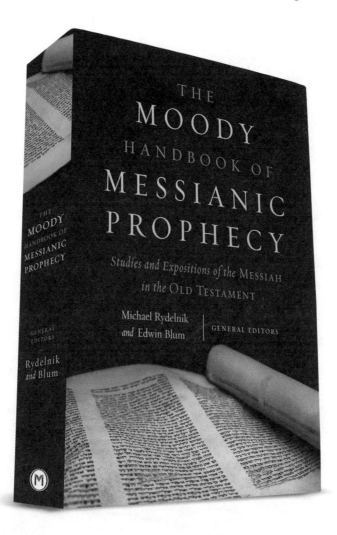

STEP INTO THE STREETS OF JERUSALEM AND ENCOUNTER THE JEWISH RABBI WHO TURNED THE WORLD UPSIDE DOWN.

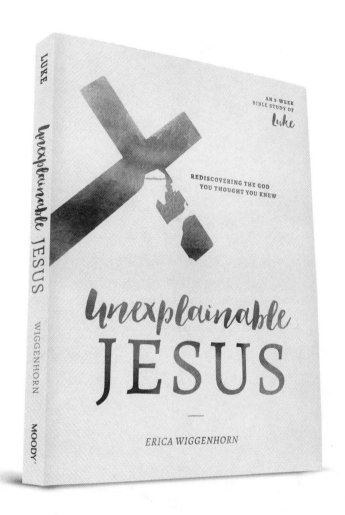

Step into the streets of Jerusalem and encounter the Jewish rabbi who turned the world upside down. After rediscovering Jesus on the pages of the book of Luke— or maybe discovering Him for the very first time—you'll see there is no other plan, goal, ambition, or person worth following but Jesus.

978-0-8024-1909-5 | also available as an eBook